Mastering User Stories

Venkadesh Narayanan, MBA, CBAP®, PMI-PBA®, CPRE-FL, CBPP
Principal Consultant at Fhyzics Business Consultants Pvt. Ltd.
Former Indian Civil Servant [IRAS 2000]

Second Edition

I0390411

Published By
Fhyzics Business Consultants Private Limited
Level-5, Tamarai Tech Park, TVK Industrial Estate
Guindy, Chennai, INDIA 600032
www.fhyzics.com

About Author

Venkadesh Narayanan was born in Tirunelveli town in Tamilnadu, the southernmost state in India. He received his mechanical engineering degree from Institution of Engineers (India) and MBA from Hult International Business School, Boston, USA. Venkadesh is a former member of Indian Civil Services and served Indian Railways between year 2000 and 2008 in capacities such as Divisional Finance Manager and Senior Financial Advisor. He also worked for various companies both in India and USA such as Larsen and Toubro, Euro-Pro Operating LLC etc. He founded Fhyzics Business Consultants Private Limited in the year 2007. Fhyzics specializes in business analysis, business analytics and SME consulting. Venkadesh has over 20 years of experience in Consulting, Business Analysis and Process Improvement and currently serving as Principal Consultant at Fhyzics. He is an avid reader and writer and penned down numerous books and articles in the area of business analysis, business analytics, process improvement, supply chain and new product development.

He holds certifications such as
Certified Business Analysis Professional (CBAP®), IIBA®, Canada
Certified PMI-Professional in Business Analysis (PMI-PBA®), USA
Certified Professional in Requirements Engineering (CPRE-FL), IREB®, Germany
Certified Packaging Professional, IoPP, USA
Certified Business Process Professional, ABPMP, USA
Certified in Production and Inventory Management (BSCM), APICS, USA
Certified in Lean from Society of Manufacturing Engineers, USA
Certified in Six Sigma from Motorola University, USA
Certificate in Hospital Management, Sankara Nethralaya, Chennai

Venkadesh is very active in LinkedIn and would be glad to get connected with you. You can visit his profile at http://in.linkedin.com/in/venkadesh or reach out to him at VenkadeshN@fhyzics.net.

About Fhyzics

Fhyzics Business Consultants Private Limited (www.fhyzics.com), a leader in business analysis, business analytics, process improvement and SME consulting. Fhyzics is an Endorsed Education Provider (EEP™) of International Institute of Business Analysis (IIBA®), Canada and Registered Education Provider (REP) of International Requirements Engineering Board (IREB), Germany.

Fhyzics serves its clients both in India and abroad in Automotive, Banking, Construction, Education, Engineering, Entertainment, Healthcare, Hospitality, Information Technology, Insurance, Manufacturing, Public Sector, Retail, Telecom and Travel sectors.

Fhyzics offers best in class training in business analysis, business analytics, lean and six sigma both in-class and video conference formats. It helped several organizations in India and abroad to setup business analysis centre of excellence (BACoE) and trained numerous business analysts to attain CBAP®, PMI-PBA® and CPRE credentials. You can visit our course website at www.bacourse.com.

Fhyzics entered into a Memorandum of Understanding (MoU) with Confederation of Indian Industry-Institute of Logistics (CII-IL) to appoint assessors for CII-IL WAREX certification, which measures the supply chain efficiency of the assessed organizations.

Table of Contents

1. What is business analysis?

Business analysis is about recommending solutions to the organization. In the course of business operations, organizations will come across certain need, problem and opportunity. The role of the business analyst is to recommend the solution to address that need, problem and opportunity.

International Institute of Business Analysis (IIBA®) – BABOK V2 defines Business analysis as *'the set of tasks and techniques used to work as a liaison among stakeholders in order to understand the structure, policies, and operations of an organization, and to recommend solutions that enable the organization to achieve its goals'.*

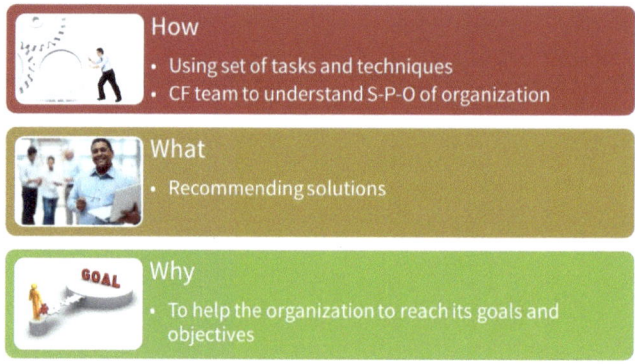

I would like to clarify here that solution and deployed solution are two different things. The former is abstract and the latter is concrete. If I hold the requirements specification document or the technical drawing of a smart phone, then I am having the solution for a smart phone. On the other hand, if I hold a real smart phone in hand then it is called as a deployed solution. So as a business analyst, I recommend the solution (provide requirements specification document) to the organization. A business analyst is performing an advisory role in the organization, so he don't implement or invest or decide, but recommends the solution.

Solution has the potential to change the state of the organization. Solution is capable of changing an organization from its current state to a desired future state. Current state of the organization is the depiction of how the organization is functioning today. In the current state there is a need or problem or opportunity. Hence the organization aspires to reach a future state where these issues are addressed.

Business analyst uses tasks (knowledge areas), techniques and underlying competencies to work with their stakeholders to understand the structure, policies and operations of the organization. Once the business analyst along with the stakeholders has a good understanding of the problem through elicitation and requirements analysis, the business analyst recommends the solution. This recommended solution is to help the organization to attain its goals by satisfying a need or solving the problem or capitalizing an opportunity.

2. What are user stories?

Let us first understand the difference between 'need' and 'requirement'. Need is a vague statement that expresses the want of an individual or an organization. On the other hand, requirement is a precise statement that expresses that want.

I am not saying that need is an unnecessary thing. Need is the starting point. Someone, somewhere in the organization has a want. Through need the stakeholder expresses the want. But the issue with the Need is, it could be understood/interpreted by different people in different manner. People fill their own assumptions in the need statement to make it complete. For example, take this need statement "I want hot water". This need statement could be interpreted by different people differently in terms of the degree of hotness (say 70 deg C), the quantity of water (say 10 litres) and when it need to be delivered (say at 10:10 am IST). So if I include all the above aspects in this example, I would be able to transform this need statement into a requirement.

So the requirement will read as "The system shall deliver 10 litres of hot water at 70 degree centigrade at 10:10 am IST". The understanding we need to arrive here is, we can start with the need statement that is fine, but we should not develop something with the need statement. First it should be transformed into a requirement and then that requirement will form the basis for all developmental work.

What happens if I go after the need statement and fully develop software or machinery? There is a rarest of rare chance that I will deliver what my customer is looking for. Meaning it will be sure shot failure that I will deliver something which is completely different from the expected software or machinery. The result is customer dissatisfaction and failed project.

Now we know that requirement is the one that forms the foundation for system development but it starts from need. The product development lifecycle (PDLC) also known as software development lifecycle (SDLC) starts from the need and ends with the developed product. The need to requirement transformation happens through business need, stakeholder need and solution requirements.

Business need expresses the wants of the business. It is a macro level one and doesn't delve into details. It doesn't talk about what the stakeholder wants or what a department wants. Business need provides a high level scope for the project. Within this framework of business need we then develop the stakeholder needs. The stakeholder need expresses the wants of users, customer, regulator etc. Hence the stakeholder need is subservient to the business need. "Dear stakeholder, you can ask me whatever you want as long as it is within the business need".

User stories is a wonderful technique to capture the business needs and stakeholder needs. In a typical project, I would get the business needs from the sponsor and the top-brass of the client and the stakeholder needs from all others who are either impacting the project or impacted by the project.

So what is a user story? User stories are statements that help us to elicit, organize and document business and stakeholder needs. User stories capture the imagination of a user as to how he is going to interact with the proposed system. It helps the user to express his intention why he wants to interact with the system and what is the benefit he is expecting out of this. User stories also help us to understand how the user wants to interact with the proposed system. An example user story: "As a driver, I turn the ignition key of my car to start the engine". This user story explains who is interacting with the system, how he wants to interact and what the benefit of that interaction is. So a simple template for writing user story is who (the user) – how (the interaction) – what (the benefit).

Who – The user	How – The interaction	What – The benefit
As a driver	I turn the ignition key	To start the engine
As a driver, I turn the ignition key of my car to start the engine.		

In the entire book, I use the word need. Need is the source of all projects and business analysis activities. When I mention need, it includes the meaning of need, problem and opportunity. Just for simplicity and to give you an easy read. In any organization, projects are kick started to satisfy a need or to solve a problem or to capitalize an opportunity.

3.Requirements & technical specification

IEEE 610.12-1990: IEEE Standard Glossary of Software Engineering Terminology defines requirement as below:

1.A condition or capability needed by a stakeholder to solve a problem or achieve an objective.
2.A condition or capability that must be met or possessed by a solution or solution component to satisfy a contract, standard, specification, or other formally imposed documents.
3.A documented representation of a condition or capability as in (1) or (2).

We have two types of analysts in organizations, one is the business analyst and the other is the systems analyst. Business analyst is responsible for requirements specification and the systems analyst is responsible for the technical specification.

The business analyst develops user stories and extracts requirements specification out of it. The systems analyst will translate the requirements specifications into technical specifications. The project manager will use the technical specification to build and implement the solution. Hence the approach follows the path: Need – User Stories – Requirement Specification – Technical Specification – Implementation.

Example of requirements specification
The system shall deliver 100 litres of hot water at 70 degree centigrade in 10 minutes.

Example of technical specification
The system shall consist of drum with lids on both ends made up of mild steel AS1594-HA250 2009 x 8mm thick plate. The drum shall be of 6 feet in diameter and 4 feet in height to hold 100 litres of hot water.
This technical specification addresses the 100 litres capacity part of the requirements specification.

4.Benefits of user stories over use cases

Developing use cases is a very formal process which takes quite a lot of time. On the other hand user stories are relatively quickly done. Use cases are very good for developing complex systems of larger magnitude, but for most of the typical software applications user stories are more than enough.

User stories are in simple English and users can easily understand during confirmation and validation compared to use cases. The user stories are written from the user interaction perspective. Hence users feel little more comfortable compared to use cases. Many a times, users are shut off by seeing use cases due to its complexity and the jargons.

In projects where the understanding of both the business analyst and the stakeholders evolves during the process of development, the changes can be easily accommodated by changing the respective user stories.

Use cases are an amalgamation of requirements. Meaning, you will write several requirements out of a single use case (say 30 requirements out of 1 use case). On the other hand, few requirements are associated with a single user story (say 2 requirements out of 1 user story).

5.A comprehensive approach to user stories

A systematic end-to-end approach helps the business analyst to develop the requirements specification document using user stories. The nine step approach from business need to requirements specification provides a template to develop user stories and requirements.

1.Define business need
2.Identify stakeholders
3.Prepare for user stories
4.Elicit user stories
5.Document user stories
6.Verify and validate user stories

6. Define business need

Business need is exposed in an organization in two ways. Either one of the stakeholders expresses a need or a problem or an opportunity that should be addressed or the business analyst may identify the need. For example, a VP (Customer Service) may initiate a business proposal and send it to the top management to address the increasing product defects and resulting customer complaints and dissatisfaction.

As a business analyst whenever we are presented with a business problem, we should first ask the question, Is it a problem or a Symptom? Many a time our stakeholders will express symptoms and call it as a problem.

Problem is the root cause of the issues the organization is facing. Symptoms are the external manifestation of the problem. Symptoms are easily visible and overt, but problems are deep underneath. If we go after the symptoms the problems will remain the same and we will never address the problem. Over a period the problem may further worsen and keep throwing new symptoms. Hence as a business analyst we should address the problem. If the problem is defined correctly, then the problem is half solved.

Let us take couple of examples,
Doctor: Hi, what's your problem?
Patient: For the last few months, I am suffering from breathlessness, growing weakness and loss of weight.
Doctor: Please help me to understand these things. Where do you stay? What's your occupation? Do you have any family history? Are you under any medication?

The patient explained to the doctor. One specific thing told by the patient captured the attention of the doctor. That is the patient is working in a mine. The doctor suspects that the patient may be suffering due to a disease called Silicosis. Now the doctor certainly knows, whatever the patient told to the doctor as problems are only symptoms. The doctor recommends few diagnostic tests. The patient returns after few days.

Doctor: Hi, how do you feel now?
Patient: It is still the same. Here is the test report for your review.
Doctor: Your report confirms that you are affected by Silicosis. This is an occupational disease. The fine particles of sand (Silica) gets into the lungs and reduces the efficiency of the air sacks called Alveoli. Hence the problem is Silicosis. On the other hand whatever you have mentioned earlier are its symptoms. First thing you should stop working in that environment. Second, take these medications, you will feel better in about a weeks' time.

If a business analyst started working towards symptoms rather than the problems, it could result in fatally failed projects. Meaning, the requirements are incorrect, right from the beginning of the project.

Mr. Rathina Sabapathy is employed with Government of India. Few days back he was transferred on promotion from Chennai to Kashmir. So he decided to relocate with his family. In about 10 days the whole family is in Kashmir in a new apartment. The family members started complaining about pain in hand and numbness. Almost everyone said we have a problem. But Muthu Sabapathy, son of Rathinam disagreed! He said what we have is a symptom, and the problem is cold water. When they lived in Chennai there is no need for hot water for bathing or cleaning purposes. At Chennai the lowest temperature recorded in a year is around 25 deg. C as it has only two seasons – summer and hot summer! But here at Kashmir the mercury could go to sub-zero. So everyone agreed, yes we have a problem that is cold water.

7.Identify stakeholders

Identifying the relevant stakeholders is a biggest challenge. There is no one way of selecting the appropriate stakeholders for a given project. Here I am recommending two techniques which will deliver best results almost all the time. They should be used together to ensure that all the relevant stakeholders are explored. The two techniques are P-S-P approach and Stakeholder Wheel.

P-S-P Approach

P-S-P approach stands for processes-systems-people. Let us define what is a process? Process is a set of sequential activities carried out in a predetermined order to deliver value to the customers. Each organization on the face of earth has finite number of processes. These processes can be categorised under primary, secondary and management processes. Primary processes are those that are the mission of the organization. That is the very purpose the organization is in existence. Customers pay for the services rendered through the primary process. For example, treatment of patients and diagnostic services are the primary processes of a hospital. Secondary processes are those that are helping the primary processes to function in a more effective manner. Housekeeping and IT billing in a hospital are the examples of secondary processes. Management processes are those that are governing and controlling the primary and secondary processes.

Once the business analysis project is assigned to me, first I will review the list of processes that are in my organization. Then I will select those processes that will be affected by the business analysis project. Say I have selected four processes that will be affected by the proposed business analysis project. I will take all the four current process maps. And then I will review the processes.

During the process review I will identify the systems that are sitting on the process which will be affected. At the end of this exercise, I will come to know both the processes and systems that will be affected by the proposed system. Now I need the stakeholders and they are the people who have good knowledge on these processes and systems.

By deploying P-S-P technique, a business analyst will identify the key stakeholders with good process and systems knowledge. But will they form the 100% of stakeholders. Of course it is not. I may need to identify some more stakeholders from other perspectives. And where the stakeholder wheel is helpful.

Stakeholder Wheel

Each organization is working in a complex environment with players from both inside and outside the organization. Most of the internal players could be summarised as employees, investors and management. The external players are regulators, environmental activists, government agencies, vendors, suppliers etc. So the business analyst should design the stakeholder wheel according to the nature of interaction the organization has with both internal and external players. Hence a customized stakeholder wheel needs to be developed for each and every organization. The below figure indicates a stakeholder wheel developed for a hospital under National Health Service, UK.

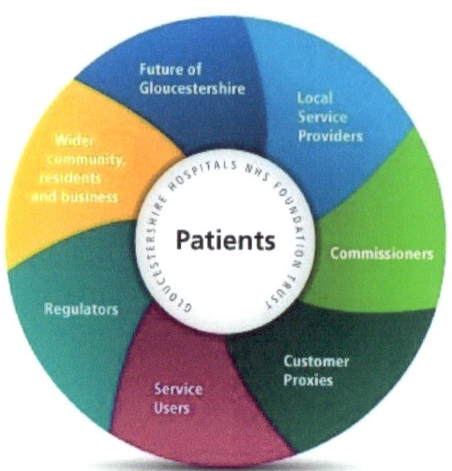

8.Prepare for user stories

It is not advisable to jump on writing user stories without adequate preparation. The preparation will help the business analyst to understand that part of the domain in a detailed manner, ask relevant questions to the stakeholders and also save stakeholders time by not asking basic questions. Document analysis and context diagram are the two techniques that will help the business analyst for a better preparation.

Document Analysis

Document analysis is nothing but going through the existing documents and literatures in the organization. This includes business plans, market studies, contracts, requests for proposal, statements of work, memos, standard operating procedures (SOP), training manuals, competitor product brochures, customer complaint logs etc. But when an organization works on a first of its kind project, you may not get much material within the organization itself. In such case one can rely on getting external support such as academic institutions, books, analyst reports (Garner, Nielson Study) etc.

Based on the business need, the business analyst should start collecting all the relevant documents that is available within the organization. Then all these documents shall be classified using ABC analysis. The most important documents should be classified as 'A' category and that constitutes 5% of the documents. The next level of importance is for the 'B' category and that forms 15% of the documents. The rest is 'C' category. The 'A' category documents should be read like a text book, 'B' should be reviewed and 'C' will be referred whenever required.

By doing document analysis, a business analyst will gain a good understanding of the business analysis area and will be able to develop better user stories and write correct requirements.

Context diagram

Context diagram helps us to separate the scope of the proposed system from the environment. The three major components of a context diagram is system boundary, use cases and actors. The system boundary separates the actors and the use cases.

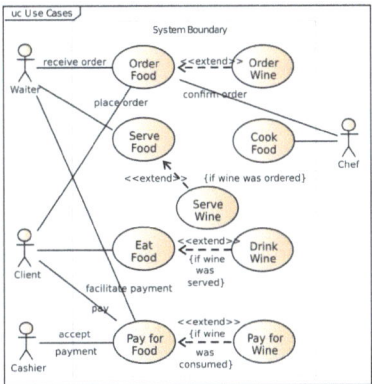

The actors (human like symbols) are the users. Actors could be humans or other systems. Actors interact with the use cases (ovals inside the system boundary). Actors want the system to perform the use case for them. So the actor who wants a particular functionality is connected with the respective use case.

Even before the commencement of elicitation, the business analysts should prepare the context diagram. This will help the business analyst to ask the right questions to understand the type of interaction the stakeholder would like to have. After all user stories explain who is going to interact, how they are interacting and what is the benefit the stakeholder want out of that.

9.Elicit user stories

Elicitation is the process of extracting required information from the stakeholders. During this stage the business analyst will meet the respective stakeholders and try to understand how the proposed system will address some of their issues and will bring new capabilities to the stakeholder or to a department. Business analyst will collect the necessary information primarily through tactfully designed questions. There are several elicitation techniques at the disposal of a business analyst such as interview, requirements workshop, brainstorming, focus groups, role playing, observation, document analysis, interface analysis, prototyping, survey, questionnaire etc. It is the responsibility of the business analyst to carefully select the appropriate elicitation technique. The selection of elicitation technique is a function of business analyst knowledge about the particular technique, available stakeholder time, location of the stakeholder, complexity of the project etc.

Elicitation is a divergent activity and not a convergent one. Meaning at the beginning of the elicitation activity there are several unanswered questions. Both the business analyst and the stakeholders are gaining a command over the business analysis area. In this stage, the business analyst seeks more and more information until he is satiated with the information. That is the point where he stops doing further elicitation.

Interview is one of the most widely used elicitation technique. During interview the business analyst meets the stakeholder in person or through other medium and collects the information through questioning. Instead of asking random questions, business analysts should use a structured way of questioning. The four stages of conducting an interview is dummy layer, scope layer, onion peeling and summary layer.

The dummy layer is to build the rapport with the stakeholder. Each of us have an unique way of communicating, known as communication idiosyncrasies. During the dummy layer the business analyst will not talk about the project but something that interests the stakeholder. This is typically for about 5 to 10 minutes. This helps both the business analyst and the stakeholder to align their communication antennas to better communicate.

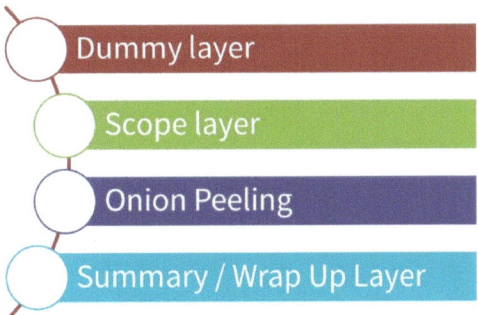

The scope layer is to present the agenda for the meeting to the stakeholder or interviewee. Then the business analyst will take one item of the agenda and will fully explore it from macro to the micro level. That is the reason we call it onion peeling. For example, I may start the interview at the process level and will end the discussion with the form fields and validation details.

In the summary layer, the business analyst will wrap up the meeting. He will indicate any upcoming meetings, what he owes to the stakeholder, what the stakeholder owes him such as reports, the preparation required from the stakeholder etc.

While conducting elicitation for user stories some special precaution need to be taken. The recommended way of questioning the stakeholder is as below:
-Do you have any role to play in the proposed system?
-Will you be interacting with the system?
-If so, what's your role and what you do?
-What would you like to accomplish by interacting with the system?
-Will you be interacting with the system only in this role or any other roles?
-What are all the non-functional elements that you can think of?
-The solution what you are recommending is fine, but tell me why you are thinking of this solution?

The elicited responses are compiled in a document called 'Elicitation Reports' and shared with the stakeholder from whom it is collected. Elicitation reports are also known as Minutes of the Meeting. Typically an elicitation report consists of the following details:
-Date of elicitation
-Participants in the elicitation meeting
-Documents shared during the elicitation
-Questions and the responses by name
-Reference materials
-Unresolved or unanswered questions
-Follow up items etc.

10.Develop user stories

Experienced business analysts will write the user stories during the elicitation itself. But it may not be a good practice as the business analyst will overload himself with too many activities. The better way to do is to gather all the information in the elicitation reports and use it as an input to develop user stories. By doing so, the business analyst will have more time to organize his thoughts while writing the user stories rather than hurriedly writing at the time of eliciting the stakeholders.

On completion of the elicitation reports, the business analyst will develop the user stories. In a way, the user stories are embedded inside the elicitation report. Words or phrases such as "I expect the system", "I want to do", "I would like to", "Being a chemist", "My role is to" etc. will indicate there is a user story hidden in the elicitation report.

We have to note one important point here. When we say user stories, it is not necessary that all the users are humans. It could also be other systems that will interact with the proposed system. Now your question is who will tell the user story for those systems. It will be formulated by the business analyst or the stakeholder by putting ourselves in the shoes of that system.

While documenting user stories care should be taken to assign appropriate attributes to the user stories to manage, store, retrieve and refer. The typical attributes are as id number, short title, author, date of creation, version, priority, severity etc. The type and number of attributes are determined by the nature of the project and report demands from your stakeholders.

The format of the user story is very simple. Going back to our previous example the user story will read as

Who – The user	How – The interaction	What – The benefit
As a driver	I turn the ignition key	To start the engine
As a driver, I turn the ignition key of my car to start the engine.		

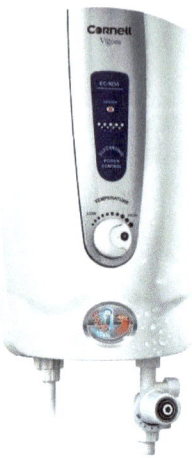

Let us develop the full set of user stories for a hot water system. Here the hot water system is the water heater. Before start writing the user stories, we need to ascertain whether we have considered all the stakeholders of this proposed water heater. The list of stakeholders include the users, the proposed system (water heater), power supply, water tank, pipeline, bathroom wall, power cables, pipe fittings, electronic equipment in the installed location, earth line, power panel, technician, service representative, switches, transporter, showroom, manufacturer, scrap vendor, water, certification, wall tile, packaging etc.

How to find out the list of stakeholders who will interact with the system? The best way to determine this is through brainstorming. Assemble few of your colleagues, may be 5 or 6 people who have good knowledge about the proposed system and from different departments. Ask the group to list out the stakeholders who may be either affecting the proposed system or affected by the proposed system. At the end of the session you will have a good number of stakeholders for your review.

User stories from the perspective of User:

-As a user, I will switch on the system to prepare hot water for me.
-As a user, I need to change the temperature setting between 30 and 80 degree C for hot water at suitable temperature.
-As a user, I need to close the inlet pipeline valve for maintenance purposes.
-As a user, I need the system to discharge 100 litres of water in 5 minutes.
-As a user, I need the system to heat the water from 25 deg C to 80 deg C in 10 minutes.
-As a user, by touching the water heater, I should not get any electric shock.
-As a user, by touching the water heater, I should not get any heat blisters.
-As a user, I should know the discharge water temperature displayed.
-As a user, the system shall notify me when the hot water is ready.
-As a user, the system shall notify me when the it is 'ON' for more than 60 minutes.

-As a system, I need to disconnect the power supply when the temperature reaches the set limit to save electricity and to avoid excessive heating.
-As a system, I need to notify when inlet water system is not working to avoid excessive heating.
-As a system, I need to notify the user when there is a choke in the outlet water system.

User stories from the perspective of Power Supply:
-As a power supply (current), I vary between 200V to 250V and the system should function in that condition.

User stories from the perspective of Water Tank:
-As a water tank the pressure level changes from 10 bar to 5 bar and the water heater should be able to function with that variation.

User stories from the perspective of Pipeline:
-As a pipeline, I am made of steel so there shall not be any electricity and heat leakage to the pipeline.

User stories from the perspective of Power Cables:
-As a power cable, I am designed only for transferring up to 2000 wattage.

User stories from the perspective of Electronic Equipments:
-As an electronic equipment, I have certain requirements in the electric circuit for optimum operation.

User stories from the perspective of Technician:
-As a technician, I need to dismantle and assemble in a quick manner for reduced downtime.

User stories from the perspective of Service Representative:
-As a service representative, I need to identify each system uniquely for proper records and service.

User stories from the perspective of Transporter:
-As a transporter, I need to transport the systems in a timely and safe manner to ensure customer satisfaction.
-As a transporter, I need to handle the system while loading and unloading in such a manner to minimise damage to the water heater.

User stories from the perspective of Showroom:
-As a retailer, I need to display the system in showrooms for better sales conversion.

User stories from the perspective of Manufacturer:
-As a manufacturer, I need to minimise the cost of manufacturing.

User stories from the perspective of Circuit Breaker:

-As a circuit breaker, whenever there is a short circuit in the equipment I need to break the power supply to ensure safe operation.

-As a scrap vendor, I need to dismantle all the different materials for better scrap valuation.

-As I flow through the pipeline and the water heater, I may deposit salt on the walls and create a clogging condition which reduces the efficiency of the water heater.

-As a certifying body, I need the water heater to meet certain safety and energy criteria to be certified as the safe and efficient equipment.

-As a wall tile, I can withstand a maximum temperature of 90 deg C, exceeding which my top layers may peel off and give an ugly look.

-As a package, I need to protect the water heater during transportation and handling to minimise the damage and scratches on the equipment.

www.ingramcontent.com/pod-product-compliance
Lightning Source LLC
Chambersburg PA
CBHW041120180526
45172CB00001B/357

business analyst and the stakeholder, it becomes clearly visible and the user story is suitably modified.

*** *End of Book* ***

11.Verify and validate user stories

Verification and validation are interchangeably used by many business analysts. Let us first establish the real meaning of these words. Verification is about the quality requirements of a user story. Whether the user story is written in the appropriate format and meets the standard of a good user story. On the other hand, validation is about whether the user story is the one that is demanded by the stakeholder. We have a separate section dedicated to the verification and validation of user stories.

Independent review is one of the methods to verify whether the user stories are written in a proper way and provide the necessary details to extract requirements out of that. Business analyst should make a dedicated time for this kind of independent review and question each user story why it is not correct and where it fails to deliver the correct requirement. A cautious review with good time spent will reveal most of the mistakes in the user stories.

Peer review is one of the best ways to verify whether the developed user stories are meeting the generally accepted standards of writing user stories. There is no hard and fast rule for writing user stories. The generally accepted standards are the minimal expectations out of a user story. These minimal expectations are any user story should talk about who is interacting, how he is interacting and what is the benefit out of that interaction. A review by one of your colleagues to verify whether the user stories are providing these details is known as peer review. Out of this review, your colleague (peer) may let you know the areas for improvement in terms of missing details, but he may not be able to tell you whether it is a correct one with respect to the stakeholder needs.

Process mapping: User stories are written to express the functional and non-functional aspects of the proposed system. As stakeholders are well versed with the functional aspects there will not be any oversight issue. But on the other hand in case of non-functional parameters either things are completely forgotten or the required level is compromised. It would be better to develop a detailed process maps at the activity level for the proposed system and then superimpose all the user stories on it using the user story id number. Through this one can validate missing and misaligned user stories.

You may face one or both of the following scenarios while matching the user stories on the process map:
-I am not able to place one of the user stories in the process map as there is no equivalent activity. Then either this user story is a surplus one or the process map is incomplete. But we know there is a problem to be addressed.
-There is one activity in the process map which doesn't have any corresponding user story. There is a chance for missing user story which is not yet identified or developed.

Structured walkthrough is one other technique that is helpful to validate the user stories. Structured walkthrough is a workshop where all the relevant stakeholders will be invited and the business analyst will review all the user stories one by one typically through a PPT and will ask the stakeholders to comment on that. Since user stories are plain English written in lucid format the understanding of the stakeholders are quite good and wherever there is a gap between the